THE RISING WATER PROJECT

•

Real Stories of Flooding
Real Stories of Downshifting

Compiled and with a foreword by
Ian Mowll

LOTTERY FUNDED

www.greenspirit.org.uk/risingwater

Published by GreenSpirit
137 Ham Park Road, London E7 9LE
www.greenspirit.org.uk

Registered Charity No. 1045532

Second printed edition (adapted for the GreenSpirit Book Series) 2016
First printed edition published by Ian Mowll in 2011
The individual authors credited own the copyright of their
contributions.

ISBN 9798784867759 (hardback) / 9780993598395 (paperback)

Design and artwork by Santoshan (Stephen Wollaston)
Printed by CreateSpace and Amazon

Contents

About this Book

~~~~~~

This is the seventh title in the GreenSpirit book series. An earlier printed edition was first published by Ian Mowll and created in Autumn 2011 with support from GreenSpirit, funding from the National Lottery Awards for All (www.awardsforall.org.uk), and help from the National Flood Forum (www.floodforum.org.uk).

You can find further information about the Rising Water Project at: **www.greenspirit.org.uk/risingwater**

*   *   *

Foreword

~~~~~~

Many, many years ago, there lived a king of England named Canute. Now Canute was a powerful ruler and his courtiers were always praising him. Each day, he would sit in audience and listen to his people.

"No-one challenges your supreme rule," one would say.

"You are greater than any king before you," said a second.

"The seas, the sky and the whole earth obeys your every word," cried a third.

Now the King was a man of courage and realism and he grew weary of all these foolish words. "So, you say there is nothing I cannot do?" he asked them.

"O king, you are powerful beyond measure!" his courtiers chorused.

"So," said the king with a glint in his eye, "then I will command the tide to stop! Go and fetch a chair and place it near the incoming tide".

The courtiers were puzzled that the king would want to do such a thing but nevertheless they hurried off and brought a chair just as he had asked. The king and his courtiers went to the water's edge and the chair was placed beside the incoming tide. The king sat down on the chair and looked out at the sea.

He turned to his courtiers and said, "I wish the tide to stop, will the ocean obey my command?"

The courtiers looked at each other bewildered but none of them dared to say no. At last, one courtier spoke up: "Yes, your majesty, why the whole earth does your biding!"

"Very well," cried Canute, "I command the tide to come no further! Waves, stop your rolling! Surf, stop your pounding! Do not dare touch my feet!" He waited a moment, and then a tiny wave rushed up the sand and lapped at his feet. "How dare you!" Canute shouted. "Sea, turn back now! I, the king have ordered you to stop and now you must turn back!" Another wave swept forward and curled around the king's feet. The tide came in, just as it has always done. The water continued to sweep in towards the beach. It came up around the king's chair, and wet not only his feet, but also his robe. His officers stood around him, alarmed, wondering whether he was mad.

"Well, my friends," Canute said, "it seems that I do not have as much power as you would have me believe. Perhaps you have learned that no-one is able to rule over the seas, the skies and the forces of nature."

The courtiers hung their heads and looked foolish. And some say Canute took off his crown and never wore it again.

*   *   *

Even though King Canute lived in the 11th century, this story is still very relevant today. We can imagine that King Canute represents the power of technology and materialism. And that the courtiers represent our society. So often the collective voice of our western society says that science and a growing economy can conquer all.

But as this timeless story shows, the forces of nature do not bow down to our ideas, rationalism and greed. Instead, we need to listen to and live in relationship with nature in order to have any chance of survival in the long run and to live meaningful lives.

And so this book is in two parts. The first part is about the effects of nature and contains experiences of people who have been flooded. The second part is about downshifting; how people have reduced their material lifestyle in some way, have learnt to live in relationship with nature and have increased their wellbeing. By downshifting, it is very likely that carbon emissions are reduced which helps slow down climate change and therefore the probability of future flooding.

Studies suggest that explaining the facts of global warming does not change behaviour. Even though global warming is now irrefutably acknowledged by scientists and that it is 'very likely' that global warming is human induced[1] there has been no wholesale change to our lifestyle to mitigate climate change.

So, how can change be effected? How can people be motivated to reduce their carbon emissions to make future flooding and climate change less likely? One way is to tell personal stories. Stories from people that we can understand, relate to, and learn from. And so, it is my hope that some of the accounts contained in this book will inspire us to take more action to face climate change and the environmental issues of our time.

– Ian Mowll

*　　*　　*

Reference:

1. A report of Working Group I of the Intergovernmental Panel on Climate Change www.ipcc.ch/pdf/assessment-report/ar4/wg1/ar4-wg1-spm.pdf

PART ONE

·

Flooding

Lynne Jones
Flooded in November 2009 in Keswick

Before the flooding I was on holiday with my husband in Wales visiting our eldest son. On the Monday of the week of the flooding I was concerned as it had been raining virtually every day for so long, the ground was saturated and Thirlmere Reservoir was full.

On the Tuesday I was checking the internet and could see that there was a mass of cloud going across Southern Ireland towards Cumbria, emails from the Environment Agency were also a concern. I was in tears, since the flooding in 2005 I have always been fearful of going through the loss of our home again, so I persuaded my husband to go back home. We drove back to Keswick through pretty torrential rain all the way on that Wednesday. Later that day we carried what furniture we could upstairs with help from a friend. We didn't empty the kitchen cupboards or take up the carpets as, after the 2005 floods, we had flood gates to put up at both doors and lockable covers for the air bricks so we thought we were fairly flood proof. Naively we thought that if the water looks like it might come above the flood gate we'll have time to shift more things.

The situation continued to deteriorate. The Met Office issued a flood warning and the Environment Agency predicted a flood at midday on the Thursday. That evening I exchanged a series of emails with the Fire Officer, Keswick Flood Action Group, the Town Hall and members of the Flood Response group which our Flood Group had organised to prepare for times like these. I was really concerned and so I got up several times during the night to check the situation, looking at the internet and going across the road to the river bend where the marker on the wall showed the number of centimetres the river was rising. It was approximately 20 cm per hour, at times the increase was visible as I watched for a while in torchlight.

On the Thursday morning the last email I sent out was at 10:30am: "Now we are cut off I am taking computer upstairs so lap top will not work. Hospital field filling up, I think it is spilling over by Brewery lane and into park. River about on the wall. Glug glug".

With the flood gates in place and the air bricks locked I was sitting in the front room with my husband having soup for lunch as water started to swill about the outside of the house. I looked at the corner of the carpet and thought it looked a bit dirty which was strange as I hoover it routinely. I then realised it was muddy as the water was coming in. Looking at the red brickwork at the back of the fireplace it was clear to see the water oozing through the cement around each brick. The house obviously leaked like a sieve. How little use flood gates and air brick covers are when the 1 metre floor void below the house was already full of water; the carpet had started to float.

Pictures from Lynne Jones' house
– by Lynne Jones.

New flood wall.

It was too late to save the carpets, I looked in the kitchen and the water was already 5 cm deep. Once it is in the house it comes up very fast so we had little time to get things – and it is VERY cold to stand in. We turned off the electricity and took the more expensive electrical equipment like the food mixer, toaster and so on upstairs together with several containers of water and a flask of hot water which I had organised beforehand. We also took up a bottle of wine, candles, torches and a battery radio and waited.

We sat in the bedroom bay window and looked over the river. The water was coming up fast. I saw 4 wooden legs floating by, then some more. I realised that these were park benches floating upside down and were being swept away downstream towards Workington.

As I looked at the river I knew that we were in for a huge bill and months and months of stress and anguish. We had put everything into our house; it was our home, our livelihood, our security for our retirement and hopefully our children's inheritance. I knew that the value of the house would go through the floor. I wondered why I had bought a house near a river?

The Fire Brigade asked if we wanted to be evacuated but we said "No". Outside the water was fast flowing and up to people's knees and teenage lads were running up and down the road in the water thinking it was great fun. The Police must have been fully stretched as the roads should have been closed earlier on to stop cars driving through causing a wave of water to come towards properties and, now it was so dangerous, to stop these teenage lads putting themselves at risk.

At its peak the water was 40 cm high in the house; it was

over the second stair. In the boiler room it went up to the level of the work surface.

On the Friday morning the water had subsided and we went around the streets to see if we could help others. Some people didn't get the flood warnings in time or hadn't signed up to them – it was a mess.

A Land Rover from Keswick Mountain Rescue Team drew up outside our house and asked if I was OK. I heard that PC Bill Barker had been killed when the bridge at Workington had collapsed. He was directing motorists off the bridge at the time. I did not know him personally but it was sad to hear this news.

My husband started to get in touch with some builders and I phoned up cottages that we could stay in for a while. We were a lot luckier than most, we had a nice place to stay and could be there for some months. One person had to move 9 times.

My life has changed and I have cried on many occasions. I can cope with the actual flooding of the river and the dirty water. What I can't cope with is the way you get treated afterwards. The worst bit was the builders and the people touting for business. I would lie awake for hours and often got up at 4 o'clock in the morning typing up minutes of meetings or planning how to galvanise people into action to respond to the flooding.

We came back to our house in March 2011 – that is over a year from the floods in November 2009. A year of seeing your house day by day filthy and ruined, progress to drying out and being restored – it takes so very long. When it rains I get twitchy. I look at the river and check the rainfall.

Our Flood Action Group has done much to try to resolve

the flooding issues within our small town but funding to solve these problems is badly needed. Donations would be greatly appreciated to Keswick Flood Action Group, c/o Rod Donington-Smith, Greta Cottage, Penrith Road, Keswick CA12 4JS.

*   *   *

Hazel Beck

Flooded in July 2007 in Felton, Northumberland

~~~~~~

The land around us was already saturated because we did not have a good summer. And it seemed as if it was raining non-stop for days and days. On the Friday it continued to rain all day long. I went to the nearby town of Morpeth that night to have a Chinese meal with a friend and her brother. The river Wansbeck which flows through the town was very swollen, I had never seen anything like it before – although I did not think too much about it at the time.

As the rain continued to fall all night we knew that there was a problem. So, on the Saturday morning my husband said that we will need to think about what to do about the situation.

We have 2 streams that meet in a 'v' at the bottom of our garden. And there is a stream on the other side of the road in a culvert. These all flow into the river Coquet. On the Saturday morning we saw the water creeping up the garden. And then the water seemed to start coming up from everywhere, it was even coming up through a grate in the driveway. The heavy rain continued.

By now the water was 1 foot deep all over the garden. My husband then said that we should do something. We had sandbags and we wanted to get more but everyone wanted them. We have a Motorhome in the driveway and I asked if we should do anything with it but my husband said we should start moving and saving things in the house first; soon it was too late to save the Motorhome. We live in a half bungalow, half house. So, downstairs we started to put our treasured possessions at bench height and we put some things upstairs. Our dog was upstairs and we took her to a neighbour for safety.

By midday the water was above my wellies. I could not see the ground anymore and I tripped over something and fell, my mobile phone got wet but it recovered!

We phoned the Fire Brigade and when they got near our house they could not get around the bend in the road because of the river. They got a big stick and put it in the water to see how deep the river was. It was too deep so they had to turn back and go around another way.

When at last they arrived, one of the Fire Crew saw our TV floating around and he joked that we will be able to get a big plasma screen replacement on our insurance! I think he was trying to make light of the whole situation. Anyway, they started to pump the water away, but as fast as they pumped it out, it just came back. The Fire Crew were then told to stand down and go to the nearby town of Morpeth because there was more risk of life there.

My husband went to ask if our neighbour was OK, I remember moving his prized stamp collection upstairs, the water still continued to rise.

Pictures supplied by Hazel Beck.

Other people from Felton came to have a look to see what was happening which did not feel nice. Perhaps they did not know what to do. But one stranger said that we could stay at his place if we wanted to which was very kind.

We went to stay with the neighbour who was looking after the dog; when I went to the door I saw her holding a glass of red wine and a bottle and she said "you will need this". I was so overcome that I burst into tears. We went to stay with her that night so that we were safe.

The water finally peaked at about 11:00pm on the Saturday night. When we came back to the house the next day, the water had gone. Everything downstairs including the kitchen, conservatory, living room and bathroom had been affected. The water had come up to just under the level of the light switches. You could tell from the tide marks.

The freezer must have floated around because it ended up on its back; it still worked. There was a bowl on the kitchen table with apples in it, it had floated onto the kitchen floor and amazingly the apples were completely dry. We did not lose any photos or personal items because they were upstairs. We did lose some things like books as presents but you can't be too sentimental.

During the flood there was a feeling of inevitability. It's beyond your control – so you just have to go with it. Sometimes you feel a bit like a headless chicken but what can you do? No-one from the police or council came; I felt that no-one checked up on us. But at the time, everyone in Northumberland was affected.

In Felton where we live only 3 houses and the Old Mill were damaged, not whole streets like in nearby Morpeth, so you can't expect a lot. Some people in our village may not even have known what had happened to us. For instance, the local Vicar sent a donation to Morpeth but nothing to us.

Since then, the Council have done a bit, they cut back the bushes to help the water to flow better and they checked a culvert. We had a JCB to dig out a channel for the water so that we have a fighting chance if the water comes up again. On the main river there was talk about taking out the gravel to help the flow of the river but this has never happened.

The aftermath was worse than the flood itself because we had to get everything back together. The insurance people were OK – when I heard what had happened to other people I realise that we were relatively lucky with our insurers. We had a clear out gang come to our house and they were ruthless. They cleaned out the whole place, whatever it was. Some things just needed a clean but they still cleared them out – like pots and pans. Maybe it is cheaper for them to do that and replace them rather than put everything safely in boxes with tissue or whatever to preserve them. They took photos of appliances as proof so that you could not claim for better ones.

I did my own list of what I had and what needed to be replaced. You forget things though, after 7 months you go away and then come back and realise that something is missing like a lemon squeezer. You don't realise you have so much stuff.

I am always worried about it happening again. When it rains heavily I wake up. I've even been down to the stream with a torch when it has rained a lot. I'm not a hysterical type of person but that's what I do now. I wonder if the next house I will live in will have will be on top of a hill.

Last winter was a bad one with 2 ½ feet of snow. I

wondered what would happen if it suddenly all melted? If the ground is frozen, the water would flood over it. I'm not amused by jokes about it all.

I am the secretary for our local flood group to help improve things and be prepared for future floods. Sometimes it feels like you are banging your head against a brick wall – it all comes down to money.

Regarding climate change, it seems that more places have been flooded in recent years such as Keswick and Worcestershire. There must be something afoot. We probably get the same amount of rain as before but maybe it all comes at the same time. Maybe the weather patterns are changing. We laughed last winter because it was so cold, it was minus 15 degrees and we wondered whatever had happened to climate change.

*   *   *

Mary Dhonau
Flooded many times in Worcester

I live in Worcester, a city infamous for being flooded. Worcester bridge and cricket ground is often seen on the TV during major floods. However, we don't live on an 'official' flood plain, where people at risk have something tangible like a river, stream or the sea to remind them that they may well flood. When we moved into my Victorian home, we didn't for one moment think that we would be flooded. We have been flooded on many occasions but none worse than during the 'great floods of the year 2000,' when we were flooded to a depth of over 3ft. The floodwater was not river water – it was sewage. I lived in a low spot of Worcester   and basically every time it rained a third of Worcester's sewage, both rain water and foul water passed by my home. With development more and more homes were been added to the Victorian drains and they could no longer cope, so every time it rained hard, the drains overflowed into the street and then poured into mine and my neighbours homes.

During that dreadful time my youngest son, then three

Pictures supplied by Mary Dhonau.

years old, had just been diagnosed with severe autism and severe learning difficulties. I was left reeling from the news. Having had four other healthy children, I knew nothing about autism and was profoundly shocked, as well as terrified for the future.

But I had little time to come to terms with the shock, as just days later my house was waist-deep in sewage. The ground floor of our family home was full of human waste – faeces, condoms, and other people's toilet roll. It was devastating. The smell was appalling! I remember clearly my son waking during the night and looking out of the window to see the street outside looking like a river. I felt sick, as experience had taught me that my house would be flooded again. My husband went downstairs to look and didn't come back. Once my son had settled, I went to join him. I remember seeing all my sons' toys floating in the floodwater, the sheer force of the water had upturned the toy boxes and as a result, he lost every toy he had. Our settee was floating in the water and everything sounded so eerie, a bit like it was no longer our home but a complete disaster zone, how on earth were we ever going to get back to normal. Again? I will never forget the look of despair on my children's faces when they came down in the morning to see the havoc this flood had wreaked on our home. Because of his learning difficulties my autistic son was unable to understand what had happened. This compounded our misery as he was totally bewildered and just didn't understand what was going on, or why he couldn't touch anything. He didn't understand why we couldn't go outside our front door, why we had to live upstairs or why we had to wear wellies all the time. His confusion was the hardest thing

THE RISING WATER PROJECT

of all to deal with, harder even than watching everything we owned, including my children's drawings, photographs and family videos lobbed into a skip during the long cleanup operation.

We were hit completely unprepared, and it took nine months before our home was repaired and we could move back downstairs again. And during that time I discovered that other people had stories just as hard as my own. One neighbour had what I can only describe as a carpet of poo running through her house. An agoraphobic, her home really was her castle, and her condition meant that she was unable to leave. Another elderly neighbour had recently lost her husband. The flood took all her wedding photographs too. She disintegrated.

So I took on Severn Trent Water – the company responsible for the drains in Worcester – to get them to take responsibility for the flooding. A little research uncovered that a third of all the sewage in Worcester came through one pipe – at the end of our road. Every time it rained the drains spilled out into the streets. The drainage system was clearly inadequate but my calls and letters fell on deaf ears.

So I got the support of my local MP and asked neighbours to write about their experience of being flooded. I put together a portfolio of evidence against Severn Trent and with two friends, who had also been flooded, took it to Downing Street. It was in the run up to the general election, and Tony Blair had famously targeted his campaigning at 'Worcester Woman' – a term given to the typical middle England female voter. Well, here were three very unhappy Worcester women on his doorstep – with television cameras – and he was forced to act.

His office rang Severn Trent Water, and they very quickly discovered that they were at fault – as you would, I suppose, with the Prime Minister on the case. They agreed to build a new £2 million sewage pumping station which would end 80 years of flooding to our street in Worcester. I was invited to open it, although I turned down their kind offer to name it after me!

*   *   *

Graham Styring

Flooded in July 2007 in Alderminster
– just south of Stratford-Upon-Avon

M y wife and I moved into our new house about 3 months before the flooding. Our house is part of a 9 house farm development; we live in a kind of community with all of the houses around a central courtyard. I am the Secretary of Alderminster Farm Management – my voluntary job is to look after the communal needs of the community; we have our own sewage plant and I ensure the courtyard, roof-tiles and any other communal needs are dealt with and paid for.

I am 74 years old and at the time of the flood I had just had a hip operation and was on crutches. The day before the flooding it was wonderfully hot and sunny. Early the next day the rain came and it continued to rain heavily right through until the evening. The ground became soaked.

Our house is 75 metres from the River Stour which flows into the River Avon. Water collected from steep hills on either side of the river upstream of Shipston-on-Stour and it flooded into the river.

There is a bridge downstream of us and the road is

raised on an embankment which acts as a kind of dam blocking the flow of water when the bridge cannot cope with the flow. And even though there are 4 culverts under the road to drain the water away, it was not enough and the road then acted as a kind of dam. As the rain continued, the water in the river started to rise rapidly and it flooded over the top of the road. One guy got trapped in his car which floated downstream and lodged in a copse and a helicopter had to be called out to lift him away to safety. His car was a write-off.

As we saw the water rising in the courtyard, we cleared our front room. We salvaged most of the soft stuff which we put onto bricks. We turned off all of the electrics on the ground floor. The water continued to rise and by late evening, about 10pm, there was about 1 metre depth of water in the courtyard and we had 20 centimetres of water in the ground floor of our house. Knowing that there was nothing more that we could do, we went to bed.

The next morning, when we got up, the water had all gone from the ground floor but there was mud, sludge and residue throughout. That day, as we were effectively cut off from the nearest road by the water still in the courtyard, some friends came around and 'rescued us' and we stayed with them the next day before moving into a nearby hotel for five nights.

Our new carpet was lost as was the stair carpet. The kitchen floor was a write-off and all of our kitchen appliances were condemned including our new washing machine, two built in fridges, dishwasher and a fridge freezer.

I have never experienced a flood before, for me it was a traumatic experience, so unexpected and sudden. Of the 9

Pictures supplied by
Graham Styring.

Graham Styring.

houses in the farm development, the six private properties all flooded to a greater or lesser degree whilst the other three rented from the local Alscot Estate (including the original farmhouse) survived – just. My property was least affected of the 6 private ones.

My next job was to get the insurance sorted out. This was harder than I anticipated because the insurers had failed to update our change of address (we bought the property only 4 months prior to the flooding) and were trying to respond to our first claim by corresponding with our previous address. So others in the community (and the district around) were quicker off the mark and it was several weeks before the insurers got going with my house. But eventually things started moving and the insurers were subsequently terrific; the builders came in and did what was necessary and after 4+ months living conditions were re-established. We spent some 6 weeks in total away during this period, visiting daily to check on work taking place, dehumidifiers etc and to use the phones, sleeping at home overnight as soon as was possible.

That was the good news. The bad news was that after the next year the insurance premiums kept going up until they were well over double. And the flooding excess had gone up from £200 to £4,500-£5,000 which meant that we were effectively not covered for a further flooding incident. It has taken over 3 years before we were able to transfer insurance to bring down the excess to the £200 previously available to us.

Subsequently, we have had lots of dealings with the Environment Agency, Stratford-Upon-Avon District Council and the Estate who own the three other properties.

~~~

It has been a long drawn out and still ongoing process to get agreements to allow us to create flood defences.

We had a management meeting the following January after the flood with the Environment Agency and the Alscot Estate representatives. The Environmental Agency gave us a lot of advice on how to protect the buildings. They said that the flood was a 1 in a 100 year incident. They agreed the only defence for the site would be an earth 'bund' (a bank of earth acting as a kind of dam) with a clay core to be constructed on land adjoining which is owned by the Estate, and farmed by tenants, almost totally surrounding the whole site.

Apart from the rapid rainfall and the steep hills upstream funnelling the water down towards us, the road bridge below us has a large original span plus a second smaller span built some time after the first, presumably to reduce the risk of flooding. Both are well over 100 years old. Examination after the flooding clearly showed the smaller span was so heavily silted up that it was almost totally unable to pass any significant volume of water, and we asked the Environment Agency to agree to clear the debris which had accumulated over the decades. They did not agree at first. So I consulted a Local Counsellor and, on his advice, I threatened the Environment Agency with legal action. Then they finally took action and the second span has been cleared satisfactorily. The water has risen twice since the flood and has flowed through the bridge, including the second span, so we know it works!

In addition, there are 4 culverts along the road which help to drain the water away. These were in need of repair and were fixed by the County Council and the Estate has since agreed to ensure entrances and exits to the culverts are inspected and cleared regularly.

As suggested we wanted to create a bund but the Estate would not allow it in their land. Eventually, after 2 rejected submissions (accompanied by Environmental Agency Approvals) the Estate has agreed, subject to one outstanding item, to us building a defence largely on our own gardens (to be constructed with brick walls to a specific standard and 2 floodgates) with a bund on a leased part of the Estate land. We are having to pay for legal assistance for the agreement with the Estate for ourselves and for the Estate's costs

Our latest planning application is with the Stratford-Upon-Avon District Council and we are waiting to get the go ahead – we are 8th in the queue and I have builders ready to start on 20th July .

In our community of houses, 5 out of the 6 of us are happy with the process we are engaged in. The 6th house has gone its own way and has paid out many thousands of pounds to defend against a future flood. The estimated costs are £45,000 to be shared by 5 owners.

So, for me, although the flooding itself was traumatic, it has been the aftermath of dealing with the insurance and protection against future flooding that has been the burden. My frustration is that I have been knocked back so many times when trying to get things done. I used to work in sales, not engineering but I have had to become a semi-expert in protection from flooding. It's not what I planned to do in my retirement but it's what I have had to do as a lot of the work for the community has fallen on my shoulders.

Flooding is on the minds of everyone in the community. It's a good crowd of people but we are all worried that it might happen again. Once, one of the occupants came back from France early because he was worried about a possible flood. And we all wonder when it will happen next.

*   *   *

PART TWO

·

Downshifting

Marian Van Eyk McCain
The Long Journey Home

I have never consciously downshifted. Neither have I ever knowingly *up*shifted. Although I've experienced both processes in my 75-year life journey. Looking back, I see it now in terms of *two* journeys, like two rivers that join part way downstream. One is a story of circumstance and serendipity, like the journey of a cork borne on the tide. The other is an inner, spiritual journey from ignorance to awareness. Both have led to the here and now of me, a writer of books and articles and blogs about simple living, ecopsychology and all things green.

I was just three years old when World War Two began, and living in Plymouth, which was one of the most heavily-blitzed cities in England. So I grew up with the sound of falling bombs in my ears, the damp, musty air of the Anderson shelter in my nostrils and with scarcity, rationing and 'Dig for Victory' posters. But since I knew no other normality, all these things seemed perfectly normal to me.

My childhood was a happy one, despite the war. And I took simplicity for granted. There was nothing remarkable

Creating a homestead in south-eastern Victoria, Australia.
Pictures supplied by Marian Van Eyk McCain.

about living a simple, non-consumer lifestyle because in those days, consumerism had not yet been invented. Rationing was in force and many things were unobtainable. For example, I never tasted a banana until I was nine years old. But people made do. And there always seemed to be enough to eat, especially as we grew vegetables and fruit in our backyard. Most other people we knew did the same. There were even some special treats, like the peppermint sweets my mother made out of powdered milk. She also made 'banana sandwiches' out of boiled parsnips with banana flavouring and to me they tasted delicious. Since I had nothing to compare them with, they seemed like real banana to me.

There was no TV in those days, no Internet, jet travel or microwaving. We had no telephone or central heating in our house and nobody we knew owned a fridge or a car. Washing machines were still in the future. People boiled their bathwater in a gas copper, grew vegetables in 'Victory gardens' and carried kitchen scraps to the pig bin on the street corner. Plastic didn't exist. Glass bottles were recycled. My grandmother, who was a skilled dressmaker, made all my clothes, using whatever material she could find. She used to comb the shops for good quality fabric remnants. We rarely travelled far from home and if we did we went by pubic transport. Almost everybody's eco-footprint was small, back then.

When the war finally ended and the troops came home, jobs were scarce and wages low. So in 1947 my family downshifted to an even simpler life. We moved to a house half a mile from a rural village in Hampshire. The house had no mains water and no indoor toilet. But being on half an acre it had many mature fruit trees and ample room for vegetables, soft fruit, pigs and chickens. Simplicity, there, was born of financial necessity, but although money was scarce, we lacked nothing. We had plenty to eat and even took apples to sell in the market. My life felt rich, full and especially wonderful because the war was over and I loved the countryside.

After I grew up and left home I shared an apartment in London, earning enough for rent, food and little else. I went on living simply because I knew no other mode of existence. However, just as a fish has no concept of water, I had no *concept* of simple living, back then. Words like 'sustainability,' 'environmentalism' and 'downshifting' were not in anyone's vocabulary in the 1950s.

But over the next two decades, without noticing it, most people began subtly upshifting, including me. As my wages improved, I bought more stuff. Returning from my first overseas holiday, I brought home four pairs of new Italian shoes yet thought nothing of it. We were all like sleepwalkers, walking through a process that hadn't yet reached our conscious awareness. Gradually, without noticing what was happening, we were being seduced into believing that the more 'stuff' we had the happier we would be. With the post-war resurgence of industrialism, as the factories switched back from making bombs to making cars and global trade re-developed and gathered force, advertising was starting to shape our lives, subliminally convincing us that our wants were really needs.

In 1965, by which time I was living in Australia – having migrated there in 1958 under the £10 scheme – I left the workforce to become a stay-at-home housewife and mother.

Marian Van Eyk McCain. Picture supplied by Marian Van Eyk McCain.

By 1969 I was living a typical suburban lifestyle in a typical suburban house, with all the 'stuff' that is seen as a normal part of suburban living. Except that we owned no vehicle. We were near the shops and well-served by public transport so remaining carless was easy and saved us lots of money. Since I had never owned a car anyway, I felt no lack.

We saved money in other ways too, such as buying everything for our babies second-hand, except nappies (which naturally were cloth as disposables weren't around yet). My then husband had spent his own childhood in Nazi-occupied Holland and living simply and as frugally as possible came naturally to him also. So we were not wasteful consumers. But our thrifty habits came from the desire to save money rather than from any commitment to the ideal of simplicity.

It was through wheeling my children to the shops in their battered old pram that my wake-up call came. Fruit flies had been (allegedly) spotted in the area and our local Council started compulsorily spraying poison around the streets, right at the level of young bodies in prams. I was incensed. So were my neighbours. We got together, protested and got the spraying stopped. I read Rachel Carson's *Silent Spring*. That, for me, was the turning point. That was when I first became conscious of the impact humans were having on our planet.

By 1971, more green books had started appearing and I devoured them eagerly. Friends of the Earth published their *Environmental Handbook* that year (I still have my ancient, yellowed copy). I went on to read *Diet for a Small Planet* and then, the following year, *Only One Earth, The Limits to Growth*, and *Blueprint for Survival*, followed in 1973 by *Small is Beautiful.* I was reborn as a greenie with the beginnings of conscious, global awareness.

Fast forward two decades. My children were grown. I had divorced and remarried. Duane Elgin had published *Voluntary Simplicity*, John Seymour had inspired a new generation of 'back to the land' visionaries and I was striding around in my gumboots in a recently-purchased thirty acre paddock in south-eastern Victoria, making mud bricks, building a composting toilet, installing solar panels, planting trees and following a long held dream of establishing a homestead in the bush. But of course we needed a four-wheel drive vehicle to get to our front gate. We bought yards and yards of polypipe to bring water from the dam down to the orchard and the vegetable garden and more yards and yards of it – plus a pump – to bring water up from the creek when the rains stopped falling and the dam began to dry up.

Although we used mud to build the walls and recycled wood for the roof timbers and all the doors and windows for the house came from demolished houses, we still required new rainwater tanks, a back-up generator for when there was no sunshine, an inverter to change the DC power into AC, deep-cell batteries...and on and on. When I add up all the energy it cost to manufacture and transport everything we needed, plus the petrol for the Landcruiser, pump and generator, suddenly rural homesteading doesn't seem quite as straightforwardly green as you might imagine – in the short term, anyway.

In fact, when I looked back, it seemed that our previous lifestyle in a small, 19th century brick terrace house in Melbourne's inner city might actually have been greener.

Creating a homestead in south-eastern Victoria, Australia. Pictures supplied by Marian Van Eyk McCain.

There, we had needed no car. I always walked or bicycled to the shops. We could walk downtown or catch a tram. Heating bills were low since terrace houses – especially those well-built 19th century ones like we had – stay warm in winter and cool in summer.

Since then we have experienced several more varieties of simple living. For example, we spent two years living in a downtown San Francisco apartment. When we moved into it, we bought the bare necessities of furniture, crockery, cutlery etc. from the Salvation Army store two blocks away. And when we left we simply called up the Salvation Army to bring their truck and take it all away again. Water-filled radiators were an economical form of heating, since several dozen apartments shared the one system. And once again the downtown location made car ownership unnecessary.

We also lived for a while in an intentional community by the shore of a lake in the Texas hill country. There, life was simple by virtue of the fact that almost all resources were shared. And once again, much of the food was home-grown. Now, we live in a very small, 18th century cob cottage at the edge of an English village – just 350 square metres of living space but ample for our needs. The 18" thick walls keep us snug, the garden provides a lot of our food and the firewood for our woodstove comes from fallen trees on a nearby estate, sawn into logs by the groundskeeper. We have no TV, washing machine, dishwasher or microwave, though we do have computers and use them constantly. We own no vehicle except a bike and our travel beyond the village is by bus and train. We buy everything locally and support our local suppliers, artisans and craftspeople. In the 13 years we have lived here we have never shopped in any of the supermarkets. And I am happier than I have ever been in my life.

Each place, each version of simple living that I have experienced in my 75 years has taught me new lessons about trade-offs, carbon calculation, and all the nitty-gritty pros and cons of downshifting – useful knowledge for passing on to others. Which is why I now write books about it.

But I also write a lot about green spirituality. Because above all, the conscious embrace of a simple, sustainable way of living, regardless of its form, has been for me a spiritual journey. It has deepened my identification with – and my profound delight in – Planet Earth and all her creatures. And it has brought me more happiness, more peace and more contentment than I would ever have thought possible.

*   *   *

Marian Van Eyk McCain, BSW, M.A., is a retired psychologist and the author of seven books, including *The Lilypad List: 7 Steps to the Simple Life* (Findhorn Press, 2004) and *Downshifting Made Easy: How to Plan for your Planet-friendly Future* (O Books, 2011). She edited the anthology *GreenSpirit: Path to a New Consciousness* (O Books, 2010) and is also a free-lance writer, columnist, blogger and co-editor of GreenSpirit Magazine. She lives in Devon. www.marianvaneykmccain.com

Jane Faith

Downshifting in Wales

I moved 21 years ago from a terraced house in London to a small, crude farm labourer's cottage in a very rural part of West Wales with 1.5 acres of land, 4 miles from the nearest town, and then after 7 years to this eco-community, where I have lived for 13 years in a low-impact roundhouse, the last 7 being semi-retired from full community living.

Since leaving London I have not had a fridge or a washing machine. I have never missed a fridge: although I like to have stores of dried beans, porridge, sugar for jam-making etc and put a lot of thought into preserving apples, strings of onions, potatoes etc that we grow, I truly prefer to keep the spare packet of butter or bacon in our small clay pot on the earth floor. Fresh fish has to eaten the same day. Yoghurt keeps fine for several. I really don't like it when I open a city fridge full of multiple choices of food, all seeming to me half dead in their state of suspended animation. So that bit of downshifting was easy for both me and my husband. We didn't have fridges when we were children either and

Downshifting by Jane Faith
including a pictures of Jane.
Pictures supplied by Jane Faith.

don't like the noises they make. I hate the noise of washing machines too, but did miss one at first, when my children were still at home. They had to learn to wash their own clothes for themselves by hand, which was a bit hard on them, I now realise, along with all the other new changes. In fact, I think that would be my main warning to people contemplating downshifting – you should really think a lot and talk a lot about it with your children. It's probably not a good idea to move them when they've just started secondary school, as my younger daughter had, especially to a different country, which Wales actually is.

Before moving we went on a Permaculture course. I would strongly recommend this as it puts you in contact with a good network of people on a similar path and supports you mentally, practically and socially when you lose touch with why you're putting yourself outside the 'normal' way of life of a lot of people you meet who don't really understand.

As we get older, coppicing, sawing up and chopping all the wood we need with double handed saws – we do not use chainsaws to break into the tranquillity – not to mention moving logs about, on often muddy paths, becomes more tiring for us, but still preferable to doing indoor work to pay for fuel. Having wood fires seems an essential for life now, and not seeing flames a serious deprivation. The smaller your house the easier to heat (and less space to need cleaning). I am happy not to have gas central heating with boilers turning themselves on and off, vents humming etc.

We do have running hot water, from the back boiler on the woodstove, and could have under floor or central heating from one too if we wanted. But we don't have any gas, oil or electricity bills. Hooray! Just saw blades to buy and tools to keep them sharp.

We have come to enjoy the seasonal variations of electric power – on short winter days there's no wind or sun, we have to go easy on the 'lecky': only watch half a DVD film on the computer or there's none left for reading in bed.

LED lights are great especially now that they come in warm colours, we can get many more hours of light now. But some candlelit nights still occur, and are enjoyable – as well as giving us extra sleep.

Even though we live quite a low-impact way I still often feel quite upset by being part of our awful human over consumption of nature, using packaging, metals, especially aluminium: which I want everyone to know we must stop using to stop consuming the soil of indigenous people in Orissa. When I first moved to Wales I was more hardcore and would rarely go in the car to events. We sold it and got a milk float, which was fun, but very limiting, and we became dependent on others for lifts. Now we drive a bit more, as part of a society that works like that, but expecting, hoping, that the peak oil price rises will gradually and soon change this way of life that we are used to. I also had a phase of only cooking barley instead of rice, split peas not lentils, as they grow in the UK, but have slid back now.

For me downshifting was right down – to no bills, no mortgage, just council tax and a car to sustain with money. This meant time to grow veg and cut wood, and less time needed to earn money and doing things I enjoy that earn less money. More time to think, to wander in nature, more freedom. It's definitely the right exchange for me. But most importantly, it just feels right, feels natural. All the people that I know who live this way do not seem to hanker for more 'comforts'. Some of my neighbours have lived happily for years with even less than we have, no electricity for instance, so no artificial music or computer, only singing and acoustic instruments, no inside taps or bath, only outside hot tub. So we live a high-tech life by comparison. Sometimes I need to retreat from it to my den where there is no silent hum of batteries or water waiting to escape from taps, just total peace – except when they're cutting silage into the night on the farm across the valley, tractors thundering on with great headlights beaming or using chainsaws at dusk in their woods! Or our other low impact neighbours are having a big party band outside with microphones fed by their big efficient windmill!

There are many ways of downshifting. Most teenagers aren't that into it – they have other agendas for the moment. Maybe while they're still with you it's best to just have downshift holidays, for them to experience simplicity, but younger ones can adapt, I think, pretty well. The only other problem that we have with this way of life is having relations to stay. We would love family to come, but can't provide facilities that they would take as basic – indoor toilets, separate bathroom, mud-free paths and it is a real pity that they don't come more often for longer, as there is so much nature here to enjoy.

One of the funny things is when salesmen on the phone try to sell me things they think I might need like house insurance and I try to explain. Another one is how visitors from 'normality' always assume we must be very cold in winter in our 1-room wooden house when, in fact, we are warmer than big stone houses.

When we meet up with friends we chat about ecobuildings, roof materials, wood-gasification stoves and sources of second hand windows rather than what's on telly.

I love going to music and dance camps in the summer but it is so hard to leave our beautiful corner of nature and especially all my vegetable seedlings to be cared for by someone else. Leaving my garden is like leaving my family. It's great once I get there – much more nourishing than flying abroad for a holiday.

It was easier to go away when we were part of a community, as responsibility for veg-growing, goat milking etc was shared and no-one was indispensible. I recommend those going into any type of farming to go as a group so that you are not tied to the farm.

*　　*　　*

Jane Faith lives with her partner in Wales. To find out more about her lifestyle, go to www.thatroundhouse.info.

Claire Appleby
Downshifting as Self-Expression

L ook up downshifting on the internet and you will find a range of definitions. Most reflect the principle of giving up something of lower value in order to gain something of higher value. The process of giving up is variously described as reducing one's standard of living, becoming less materialistic, consuming less, simplifying one's lifestyle, or giving up all or part of one's work and income. What is gained is an improved quality of life, a more balanced, healthy and slower paced life, a more environmentally sustainable life with a reduced ecological footprint, more time for the important and enjoyable things such as leisure or time with the family, more meaningful work and "daily lives that line up squarely with [our] deepest values" (Schor 1998[1]).

To me it is this last point that is the most important. Regardless of what you give up, and what you replace it with, what is most important is that you create a life that enables you to express your true self and your most deeply held values – in effect, to be yourself.

Claire Appleby at work. Picture supplied by Claire Appleby.

Downshifting doesn't have to be a one-time decision. A gradual shift is just as good, if not better. This has been my experience of downshifting. I probably started around 1994 and am still working my way 'down'. An important trigger for me was the desire to study for a PhD. However, since I had always worked in the environmental sector, and only acquired my first permanent and moderately well-paid post in 1990, this shift was not the conventional change from high paid work and excessive consumerism. I had been raised in a family with a love of the natural world, a modest, but comfortable, lifestyle, and a limited interest in consumer goods. Holidays were spent walking, bird-watching, brass-rubbing, reading and talking, all activities that required few funds after the initial purchase of basic equipment such as binoculars. This led, naturally enough, to me choosing a career related to wildlife and nature conservation, which, in those days, offered few opportunities beyond poorly paid short-term contracts. As a result, my 'upshifting' was very gradual – it took me fifteen years to get my first permanent post!

While I gradually worked my way up the career ladder, acquired my first house and slowly filled it with possessions, I nevertheless intuitively made decisions that reflected the values laid down during my childhood. Without making a conscious decision to buy things made from natural materials, I was instinctively attracted to them. I preferred wildlife gardening to a more formal style, avoided chemicals in both house and garden, and worried about using too much of resources like petrol, water and energy. At the same time, the intellectual challenge of work was more important than the pecuniary rewards, so I chose lower paid jobs where these were more interesting than better paid opportunities.

My two main areas of interest were the natural world and the broad area of ideas encompassed by philosophy, religion and spirituality. These two threads came together when I discovered shamanism, initially through the writings of Kenneth Meadows, with whom I later studied. I became increasingly interested in the relationship between humans and the natural world in shamanic societies, and I wanted to explore this for lessons that might be relevant to our industrialised society. Realising that this could be a 'new age' project or something more serious, I felt that studying for a doctorate would provide valuable structure and foster serious research. My boss at the World Conservation Monitoring Centre, where I worked full-time, refused my request to reduce my hours, and my pay, by half (saying that they had far too much work for me to do) so I resigned. This is the only time I've made a really big change in my gradual downshift, and in that first year I did some teaching, earning a mere £4,500 while paying part-time tuition fees of £1,500 to Sussex University, where I had registered for my PhD studies.

While my change in employment brought a lower income, which encouraged me to rethink my spending, it also, and perhaps more importantly, led to a more flexible lifestyle. Instead of working in an office five days a week, I combined teaching commitments at several colleges with home-based preparation and my PhD studies. Such a 'portfolio career', where people choose several different jobs, often with a combination of employment and self-employment, is adopted by many downshifters.

For many people it is this shift to a flexible pattern of working that opens the door to a lifestyle that allows full self expression. When I worked full-time I lived near Cambridge because that's where my employer's office was located. When I was no longer an employee I was free to move away from the heavy traffic and dual carriageways that encompass the city, and to choose a village large enough to provide facilities and a thriving community but small enough to feel friendly, relaxed and rural. Working from home I no longer have to drive to work, and I have swapped the uninspiring office environment of humming computers, Formica desks and inadequate ventilation for a timber-framed and lime-plastered office with doors opening onto an abundantly overgrown garden and a large dog lying patiently at my feet. Exploring new areas of work, I increasingly focus on those that I really enjoy, and that allow me to exploit my existing talents or to develop new skills that excite me. Enjoying the company of creative people, and being inspired by their stories, I chose a niche that allows me to spend time with those people and, increasingly, I choose work that allows me to read about, write about and talk about the things that I am passionate about. With the flexibility to express my own core values I find I am more focused in the present and the local. I no longer have a television or buy a newspaper, but increasingly engage in local initiatives such as the parish council, community farm and community woodland, reflecting core values that include interconnectedness, empowerment, community and caring. Through these activities I meet people who share my values and, through our involvement, these local initiatives evolve to reflect those values. The concept of work-life balance no longer makes sense because it is all 'life', with a varied mix of activities, some of which I happen to get paid for. And I don't think too much about how much the work pays because somehow it all works out, mainly because I spend very little since my recreation comes directly from the work I do and the community activities that I'm involved in.

My interest in value-driven lifestyles, of which downshifting is an example, developed when I extended my portfolio career by training as a life coach, specialising in 'slow' living and quality of life. Helping clients to identify and express their core values enables them to draw on their inner resources and become more resilient. They find fulfilment in the expression of their true selves rather than relying on external endorsement from a society that doesn't share their values.

*   *   *

Claire's website can be found at www.the-slow-coach.co.uk

Reference:

1. Schor, Juliet B (1998), *The Overspent American: Upscaling, Downshifting and the New Consumer*, Basic Books, New York

Sally Lever
Downshifting in the West Country

Twenty-two years ago, I wasn't even aware of the term 'downshifting'. Initially, it was more of an inner shift rather than a downshift, a return to common sense and to listening to my heart that triggered the change and that drove me towards a radical change in lifestyle.

After giving birth to my first child in 1989, I sensed a change in attitude towards work and towards materialism. Becoming a Mum seemed to put me back in touch with what was really important to me in life – my values. Family life had always featured strongly for me, but in this instance I simply could not bear to put money-earning and personal status above spending time with my baby, whatever the consequences of that might be.

My original plan was to return to my former job, fulltime and put my baby in a day nursery. When I started researching day nurseries, there was nothing that I considered suitable that had fulltime places. It was then that I realised I couldn't face the idea of leaving him for that length of time during the week anyway. I also wanted more flexibility in my working hours. So, I decided to become self-employed and return to work part-time – just 2 days per week to begin with. This suited me fine and seemed to work well for my baby too. It did mean that my partner and I then had less salary coming in to the household, but we found that we were able to talk it through and to cut our costs so that we could manage.

In hindsight, this was the first stage of my downshifting journey. After having a second son and once both of them had started school, I was still working part time self-employed but things started not working out so well for them in school. They were both very stressed out from having to conform and from not having their educational needs met. One was also being bullied relentlessly, despite all our efforts to resolve the situation. In short, I decided to home educate them. This second shift, again prompted by a return to core values, triggered a series of events. With the children being home educated, I didn't have time to work and so sold my business. This then left us as a family with a reduced income for a second time, only in this instance we found ourselves overstretched and could no longer afford to pay the mortgage on our house. After much deliberation, we decided to move to the West Country to be nearer close family members. We also decided to use the opportunity to buy a much less expensive house. This left my husband and me with the freedom to earn less money between us and gave us both the opportunity to choose work that enabled us to do what we really enjoyed.

As with many couples, deciding to reassess our lives in an honest way meant facing some challenging relationship issues. A few years after our move to the West Country, we

Sally Lever. Picture supplied by Sally Lever.

chose, quite amicably, to part company. I've continued to downshift and our children are now quite grown up and are venturing into adulthood.

In all, I took 5 years off work while the boys were still young and needed me to be around to home educate them. As they got older, they became more independent in their education and I was itching to have some time to myself doing something more challenging. I retrained in coaching and started working, self-employed again from home just 1 day per week. I gradually increased my working hours around their requirements until they entered college, by which time I was up to 20 working hours per week.

Now, my oldest son has finished at university and has left home, while the younger one is still in college. Having spent nearly 5 years as a single parent, I remarried in 2009. I am now living with my husband, a fellow downshifting enthusiast, and youngest son in a modest sized house with a large garden, within walking distance of the centre of a major town and the beautiful Somerset countryside. We are growing lots of fruit, vegetables and herbs in our garden and are both working from home. We are eco-renovating the house and have so far completed most of the work on insulation, and installing a wood-fired alternative to the gas central heating system. This is expected to be completed this summer, with the addition of solar thermal hot water.

So far, what I most love about this way of life is having more time, flexibility and autonomy for the things that really matter to me. For me this has been as much a spiritual journey and awakening as anything else. I've realised how much of our conventional existence is dictated to us, externally by big corporations and a pseudo-democratic government and internally by my conditioning.

I've appreciated spending much more time, than I might otherwise have done, with my children during their childhood and still having time to spend with them as adults now. I'm so grateful to the many other home educating parents, coaches and therapists I've met who've taught me so much about how to live according to how I truly am, regardless of what others might think, how to educate myself and how to slow down.

There have been some extremely challenging times, particularly getting divorced, and several points where I really was not sure how I was going to survive financially. At times, I've struggled to see a way through, so I've surrendered, just trusted that I was doing the right thing and that it would all work out ok.

Overall, remembering my values and the meaning of what I was doing seems to have been what's got me through those transitions so far. Actually, I realise I quite enjoy challenges anyway! I see them as opportunities to learn, which I derive a lot of satisfaction from, in a scary sort of way!

I can put my hand on my heart and say that I miss absolutely nothing from my life before downshifting. Far from it – I feel as though I've gained so much: time, wisdom, vision, courage, love and community...I feel bemused when others view the prospect of downshifting as some kind of terrible hardship. For me, this is a wonderful blessing.

*   *   *

Sally writes about the heart and soul of downshifting to a more sustainable, ethical and holistic way of living and working, in keeping with the needs of the planet, humanity as a whole and

ourselves as individuals. She works internationally, offering 1-2-1 coaching by telephone or Skype and group workshops. You can subscribe to her blog and monthly email newsletter via her website: www.sallylever.co.uk

ABOUT GREENSPIRIT

GreenSpirit is a network of people who celebrate the human spirit in the context of our place in the natural world and Earth's own evolutionary journey. Our radical vision brings together the rigour of science, the creativity of artistic expression, the passion of social action and the wisdom of spiritual traditions of all ages. Attracting those of many faith traditions, we are a body of people who believe that human life has both an ecological and a spiritual dimension. Together we:

• celebrate all existence as deeply connected and sacred
• understand humanity as integral to the planetary landscape rather than its distinguishing feature
• find inspiration in the traditions of Earth-based peoples and Celtic spirituality
• are exploring the unfolding story of the Universe and promote common ground between people in the context of this vision
• seek to redress the balance of masculine and feminine and befriend darkness as well as light
• create ceremonies and celebrations which connect us more consciously with the cycle and seasons of the Earth
• seek a more just, sustainable and peaceful way of life in harmony with the Earth

GreenSpirit is a UK registered charity. Membership is open to everyone, details of how to join are at www.greenspirit.org.uk or write to GreenSpirit, 137 Ham Park Road, Forest Gate, London E7 9LE.

GreenSpirit runs national events and supports a network of local groups as well as producing a regular magazine and e-newsletter. GreenSpirit also has its own online social network and website where you can find out more about the Resource Pack, Book Service and Publications.

Other titles in the GreenSpirit Book Series

What is Green Spirituality? Edited by Marian Van Eyk McCain

All Our Relations: GreenSpirit Connections with the More-than-Human World. Edited by Marian Van Eyk McCain

The Universe Story in Science and Myth. By Greg Morter and Niamh Brennan

Rivers of Green Wisdom: Exploring Christian and Yogic Earth-Centred Spirituality. By Santoshan (Stephen Wollaston)

Pathways of Green Wisdom: Discovering Earth-Centred Teachings in Spiritual and Religious Traditions. Edited by Santoshan (Stephen Wollaston)

Deep Green Living. Edited by Marian Van Eyk McCain

Dark Nights of the Green Soul: From Darkness to New Horizons. Edited by Ian Mowll and Santoshan (Stephen Wollaston)

Awakening to Earth-Centred Consciousness: Selection from GreenSpirit magazine. Edited by Ian Mowll and Santoshan (Stephen Wollaston)

GreenSpirit Reflections. Compiled by Santoshan (Stephen Wollaston)

Anthology of Poems for GreenSpirits. Compiled by Joan Angus

The Lilypad List: Seven Stpes to the Simple Life. By Marian Van Eyk McCain

Meditations with Thomas Berry: With additional material by Brian Swimme. Selected by June Raymond

Free for members ebook editions

73

GreenSpirit
magazine

GreenSpirit magazine is free for members and is
published in both print and electronic form.
Each issue includes essential topics connected with
Earth-based spirituality. It honours Nature as a great
teacher, celebrates the creativity and interrelatedness of
all life and of the cosmos, affirms biodiversity and human
differences, and honours the prophetic voice of artists.

Find out more at www.greenspirit.org.uk

*"For many of us, it's the spirit running through that
limitless span of green organisations and ideas that
anchors all the work we do. And 'GreenSpirit' is an
invaluable source of insight, information and inspiration."*
– JONATHON PORRITT.

GreenSpirit
Path to a New Consciousness
Edited by Marian Van Eyk McCain

Only by understanding the Universe as a vast, holistic system and Earth as a unit within it can we help restore balance to that unit.

Only by placing Earth and its ecosystems – about which we now understand so much – at the centre of all our thinking can we avert ecological disaster.

Only by bringing our thinking back into balance with feeling, intuition and awareness and by grounding ourselves in a sense of the sacred in all things can we achieve a new level of consciousness.

Green spirituality is the key to a new, twenty-first century consciousness. And here is the most comprehensive book ever written on green spirituality.

Published by Earth Books
ISBN 978-1-84694-290-7

'*GreenSpirit: Path to a New Consciousness* offers numerous healing and inspiring insights; notably, that Earth and the universe are primary divine Revelation, a truth to be transmitted to our children as early and effectively as possible.'

~ THOMAS BERRY (January 2009)

Printed in Great Britain
by Amazon

29907671R00045